the skin
of dreams:

new and collected poems 1995-2018

2019 Purple Basement Poetics
An Imprint of

Copyright © 2019 Quraysh Ali Lansana

All Rights Reserved
Published in the United States by Purple Basement Poetics
An imprint of The Calliope Group, LLC

Trade Paperback
ISBN: 978-1-7336474-0-3
ISBN: 978-1-7336474-1-0 (eBook)

Library of Congress Control Number: 2019933277

Author Photo: Two Sisters Photography

Cover Art: A Memory Long Ago. Byron M. Shen

Several poems first appeared in the following publications:

The Eloquent Poem Anthology, Persea Books, 2019: "descendent" and "echolalia"

The Girl Who Turned Into a Moth: Contemporary Poets On Autism, New York Quarterly Books, 2019: "echolalia one," "echolalia two," "flight," "trek," "the spectrum," and "golden"

Gulf Coast, Spring 2018: "higher calling"

Chicago Public Radio, Every Other Hour/InVerse, August 2017: "all talk"

The Golden Shovel Anthology: New Poems Honoring Gwendolyn Brooks, University of Arkansas Press, Spring 2017: "1972 ford ltd"

Oklahoma Today Magazine, January-February 2017: "civility"

Poetry Bay, Fall 2016: "seven years"

We Speak Chicagoese: Stories and Poems by Chicago Writers, Side Street Press, 2016: "dead dead"

bozalta, Vol. 2, Spring 2016: "letter to my deceased best friends: a work in progress"

After Hours, Issue #31, Summer 2015:" brown," "space," "weekend," "in eufala," and "a way of listening"

African American Review, Vol. 48, #4, Winter 2015: "black jesus"

Oklahoma Today Magazine, January-February 2015: "tulsa blur: 1921 to 2012"

Hyperlexia Journal: Poetry & Prose About the Autism Spectrum, 2014: "echolalia one," "golden," and "flight"

Also by Quraysh Ali Lansana

POETRY
The Walmart Republic w/Christopher Stewart (Mongrel Empire Press, September 2014)

mystic turf (Willow Books, October 2012)

bloodsoil (sooner red) (Voices From The American Land Chapbook Series, May 2009)

Greatest Hits: 1995-2005 (Pudding House Press, 2006)

They Shall Run: Harriet Tubman Poems (Third World Press, June 2004)

Southside Rain (Third World Press, January 2000)

cockroach children: corner poems and street psalms (nappyhead press, Fall 1995)

NONFICTION
Our Difficult Sunlight: A Guide to Poetry, Literacy, & Social Justice in Classroom & Community w/Georgia A. Popoff (Teachers & Writers Collaborative, March 2011)

ANTHOLOGIES
The Whiskey of Our Discontent: Gwendolyn Brooks as Conscience and Change Agent, with Georgia A. Popoff (Haymarket Books, 2017)

Revise the Psalm: Work Celebrating the Writings of Gwendolyn Brooks, with Sandra Jackson-Opoku (Curbside Splendor, 2017).

We Are: Chicago Photographs and Literature (The Chicago Community Trust, 2016)

The Breakbeat Poets: New American Poetry in the Age of Hip-Hop, with Kevin Coval and Nate Marshall (Haymarket Books, 2015)

Dream of a Word: A Tia Chucha Press Anthology w/Toni Asante Lightfoot (Tia Chucha Press, August 2005)

Role Call: A Generational Anthology of Social and Political Black Literature w/Tony Medina & Samiya Bashir (Third World Press, 2002)

Glencoe/McGraw-Hill's African American Literature Reader (Glencoe/McGraw-Hill, 2001)

dream in yourself: A Collection of Literary Works from Chicago's award-winning youth arts employment program, Gallery 37 w/Jenn Morea (Tia Chucha Press, 1997)

I Represent: A Collection of Literary Works from Chicago's award-winning youth arts employment program, Gallery 37 (Tia Chucha Press, 1996)

CHILDREN'S LITERATURE
A Gift from Greensboro (Penny Candy Books, 2016)

The Big World (Addison-Wesley, 1999)

for the brotherhood:

Russell Leon Hutchison (1964-2001)
Michael Tod Lilburn (1964-2006)
Joe Kollman

&

the purple basement familyhood
(ya'll know who you are)

promise kept

&

my parents:

Dorine Myles (1932-2005)
Willie C. Myles (1929-2002)

the skin of dreams: new and collected poems 1995-2018

Table of Contents

They Shall Run: Harriet Tubman Poems (2004)

Southside Rain (2000)

Cockroach Children (1995)

new
poems
(2018)

1972 ford ltd

"Their country is a Nation on no map."
from The Blackstone Rangers, II The Leaders

a harvest gold & avocado green leisure suit with fm radio, it was their,
well, daddy's, mansion, his james brown conk cool, his funky country
on radials, power windows and doors a working class music. here is
our block-long plush, envy of uncles and teenage dolemite dreams. a
ms. cleopatra jones ride, showing yankees, john denver, the hippie nation
and everyone except texas the middle finger. kept the 25 gallon tank on
full. we drove to kentucky for my sister's wedding on hot backroads, no
cracker corn farmer's rifle loud enough to make daddy use a map.

tulsa blur: 1921 to 2012

red dust simmering below skin of earth
is how bullet transcends muscle, history
a howling fire gasolined to ravenous mouth
like language, like hate. irritable june heat
in march a trigger, fuse drawn to surface

indecisive sky. gunpowder ageless
as blood, the northside of heaven ablaze.
africans tread atlantic on familiar limbs.
ninety-one year old slug lurking in elevator
shaft, bell curve, the front page of a newspaper

a senator's lips, the lynching bee, no the cries.
duped into minimum wage belief we are alive
buried in piles of our own toil, prosperity's rubble.
ancestors compelled to council, their pull stronger
than our illusion, theirs the largest mob.

brown

the papyrus of mama's dying skin
sorrow in sister's eyes
dust cloud from leaving tires
mutha's garden on bare feet
awkward first dance polyester
boley, idabel, langston

coffee pacing a hospital hallway
daddy's cowboy boots on sunday
leather that bears your name
pigskin against blue afternoon
anxious paneling in the den
the problem of sundown

in eufuala

I.
insides unsettled, shake
as elder magnolias open flanks

welcome my dna to branchless
boulevard sentries. a social club

an invitation. this is southern
heat, nigga. more humid than

oklahoma, nigga. more suffocatin'
than chiraq, nigga. mind yo mouf

nigga.

II.
this saturday eufuala will dress
antebellum, greet masses seekin'
the inside of big houses. relive
an old now (and the cotton is high).
twenty-first century realtors avoid
ghosts in their language. architecture
to admire, thirty-foot marble columns
granite countertops, coach houses.

black folk don petticoats & top hats
do the post-race chicken george.

III.
on an oppressive afternoon i crossed
431 to meet a lonely cotton field
in waiting. for rain. for a buyer.
for iron from lashed backs or neck
snap (that was mississippi, my bad).

IV.

you can put your sign in my yard
but i can't vote for you, sis told
kinfolk, holding payroll in his face.
look, she signs my checks. day before
election good ol boys rear end
his foreign sports car. he left town
two days later. *we got good niggas*
who know they place. they do.

V.

and everything is obese. even
the billboard reads a southern
super size: two diabetes biscuits
with a hot cup of cholesterol, only
two dollars. dixie battered hope
in a boiling vat of confederacy.

VI.

thought about drawing blood
blade to melanin, return my dna
to seed crusty dirt, genetic the crop.
a loud lynyrd skynyrd picnic
all the meat you can eat, plus sweet
tea. cavities in the alabama dusk.

VII.

brotha asked me to talk on
how to have your voice heard.
blacks unsure of the use. branches
on trees near the lake.

VIII.

after the talk, was taken behind
the writing center, rolled in seasoned
batter (lawry's), dumped in grease. eleven
minutes later emerged with big lips, alabaster
teeth, jockey pants, 44 raised on my back.

seven years

eight hundred miles away for two thousand
five hundred and fifty-five days blanketed
in the melanin rich cocoon of the south side.

jacob squatted in hollow of tree for one hundred
sixty-eight hours til slave catchers passed. only
duppies, good and ornery, vex me here

where it is possible to function, to dream
and never interact with a person of non-
color. more black owned businesses in

my neighborhood than my hometown. can
be thug, threat, teacher, artist, arse, poet
professor, writer, worrier. but sad nigga

in enid, my view obscured by headstones
prison and ferguson. the fools gold of distance.
damp musk of time. grief decomposes on I-44

weather lovely, the politics fucked. fracked up
earth twitches, spits greed. we drive by anyway
led by dollar signs. an uneven stretch of lonely road.

civility

the first time a friend from high school
called dad by his first name, neither
of them were troubled. neither stifled

extension of hand, smile of long knowing.
when we were young he was mr. myles.
fifteen years gone, those teenage clowns grown

men, middle aged testosterone. my friend
freshly knotted, my nuptials looming. dad
wrinkling toward casket. it was an odd sting

maybe the okie twang which i never harbored
nor appreciated. six years since daily tongue
was this country music, reminder of one-way

ticket, $23, a folder of poems. but this remains
home for them. *good to see ya, j* as they grip.
would never call his pops john to his face

or his son's, my closest homey from 1980.
i ask about his father and call him sir when
we meet. is this culture, privilege or bad

manners? my big city black fertilizing
weed where wheat and alfalfa grew. are they
dubois and me booker t.? i stand in the front

yard with men who have informed my sight.
one black, one white. i swallow. dad goes on
his way.

fiftyish i figure

after Jasper Johns

i no longer know my age
stopped counting at 50.
think I'm still here
awash in hue and shadow
of daddyhood, *a little boy*
without a friend is how franti
put it. the patina of middle
life, substance of sleeplessness
manic busy, a working artist
an artist working. an oxymoron.
somewhere lurking, hidden
in alleys of dreams, i am.
scrub sponge on my face
& cocoa butter to infant my skin.
pills to cool my blood for public safety. science
not my calling but hear her distant
trickery, slight of hand. last week
at a funeral a woman i've known
for twenty years failed to recognize
me. *you look different.* unsure
if compliment or concern.

basement blur: wisconsin

in a basement with whiskey zeppelin II & cheeseheads drunk on hail mary. could start mess but outnumbered. this is not the underground hug i long for. very far away and not. milwaukee not norman. they are not the same. i was safe there. 2015 not 1985. kindred demographics in beer flannel & guitar music. white boy infatuation with black pain. another melaninless room. outside those purple walls, oklahoma history. inside we made our own. six years in a drunken cellar without cracker syntax. a brotherhood. mostly love down here. hate across street. klan on campus. a red-eyed reagan ache. here it's packers & obama too long in charge. they okay with jay-z. sport green & gold not crimson & cream though just as fevered. fortune on the legs of black men they call nigga when game is done.

letter to my deceased best friends: a work in progress

need to talk brethren. we need to reason, as rastas do. spark
chalice or spliff, help me find sense. i'm tired, brethren. of talk
struggling with prayer, and fuck forgiveness. before i do some
thing smart or stupid. white boys whom i love greater than life
greater than myself, if you're trying to holla i can't hear you. i
know i'm in my own way but dammit i can't figure out where
to move. do i harbor any conviction as deeply as dylan storm
roof? blood kin, a handful of others and you two. they know
i would die for them and you did too. but kill? for twenty-six
years i've sworn i'd only buy a firearm for one reason, the one
this roof kid wanted to ignite. it's been a long eight months
brethren, a long four hundred years. not sure if i've lost my
mind or found it. this dude's act guts me in most things i hold
sacred: history, spirituality, respect, inclusiveness & black people.
maybe it's that i was raised ame. have an idea of all that occurred
in that hour, order of study until he emptied that clip, reloaded.
that's not part of the apostle's creed. and the families forgave him
and that's Jah and that's love and i know Jah and i've known
love and i cannot forgive him, jason van dyke, darrin wilson, cops
in cleveland, long island, waller county, jasper, a fucking pool party
rahm emmanuel, eighty-six minutes of missing video. is this letter
rant, poem, prayer, rock, slingshot, stick, blade, pistol, semi-automatic
hand grenade? sanity? tanks rolled down main street in small-town
usa, brethren. everywhere is war, marley sang. know that, for now, you
two are why i haven't. holla.

five from the pokey, or why i thought barry manilow was Jah

naah, homey, the freaky-deaky
is like this: snap your legs to the side.
man, you move like barney rubble.

about to engage in the disco lovefest of our thirteen year
old lives and russ moved like a squatty white boy
which was true, but what he lacked
in grace was covered with style.

invited to the disco room of the imperial hotel by the coolest
women at longfellow junior high school, both named christy.
we figured christy meant righteously hip in russian.

big christy had a foot on mark killiam (no joke), the biggest dude
in school. even the principals were afraid of her.

> and there was christy the bad ass rocker chick.
> she had yet to reach biker chick status, but was on
> her way. she found weed and jack daniels before
> her twelfth birthday, sometimes before class.

she thought we were cool 'coz one day in fifth hour russ and me
tied kevin byrum's shoelaces to his desk while he was meditating.

> so, christy the rocker asked us to join big christy and her manfriend
> jimmy, who was old enough to run for president. she dug him.
> here's a man willing to escort minors to the hippest, most happening

scene in enid, oklahoma. besides, our gym teacher was sexing the entire
cheerleading squad. didn't seem like that big a deal at the time. we were
jonesing for them too.

we arrive, and russ is stylin his MALE brand denim suit.
i'm puttin a power move on the mirror ball with black bell
bottoms, made from polyester, nature's wonder tool.

    really soon, we are silly
    on drink, beats and bootays.

    then a phrase drifted from the front of the dance floor
    careened off the mirror ball and hit us upside the heads.

the place is about to be raided!!!

the words hovered, laughing at the commotion.
coats, arms, legs flying wildly. russ and i grabbed
our jackets and ran across the street to a pay phone.

    "mom, will you come pick us up?
    we're across the street from the imperial."
    boy, what's all that noise?! what's going on?!
    where are you?!!!

fifteen police cars flew down van buren.
we watched the christy's as they were escorted to
squad cars and saw jimmy plead with the pigs.
so much for his political career.

and three teachers lost their jobs due to questionable
teaching methods before we graduated.

rudie can't fail in south padre

there was a rude boy on my jean jacket. black suit, shades and hat,
skanking where orange street met birmingham. two-tone ska a second
skin, a way to believe, though unsure why. days on this island with wasted
republican frat boys and sorority girls, pompous u.s citizens, northern
americanos with trust funds. only white dudes in sight without reagan hair
are in the front of the car, a sputtering nondescript, and later pugs, the
skinhead in boots and leather below unfiltered sun, unsure if peyote caps
or heat is source of glistening blister of a head. an equally overdressed
chubby blonde woman at his side who he swears sounds just like janis. on
cue, val fills the hotel courtyard where my misfit crew hope for a corner
of a floor not coated in puke or recent sex rented by bobcat's brother's
sigma hate niggas fraternity. her dense wail careens off ten stories like a
friday night public address system. so close to another why not join the
hollow migration? us, funboy three, avoiding the same people in a different
country. tequila, laughter and respect. then border patrol. stinking agave
as he checks licenses and cargo space. when he opens the back door, rudie
rests beside skinny black sophomore with a flat top. one front pocket open,
the other concealing skunk. i consider what dank brick lines the cells, how
long i will drink sweat because it tastes better than juarez prison chow. he
reaches in the open pocket, returns rudie to the seat. welcome home, boys.
enjoy yourself, he says. it's later than you think.

black jesus

there was no way not to see him. if entering the house from the front door, he smiled at eye level, locs fading into shimmering dark. if coming into room from interior hall the neon bulb seduced, effortlessly wooing to his soft gaze. swagger too much for you to pass. over a dirty white crushed velvet sofa, on which we were only allowed to sit if we had company, nailed to blonde uneven paneling, my clenched fist older sister raised black jesus to the never seen before ire of mama. blue-green shag his vexed earth. i counted days he reigned, across living room from decaying red encyclope-dias on the corner bookshelf and wall-length china cabinet uncle john henry bought overseas. one. two. after school he's still house prophet, glow kiss-ing lines on his silken face. three.

higher calling

how you, heathen passenger, gonna help the nun
sitting across the aisle on a LA bound flight
dressed in drab habit, bone scapular & bright belief
ovahstand she needs to get off the damn cell phone?
her tongue central american cataclysm & barrio Jah.
who am i to tell a mercy angel the rule she must close

her flip phone? my sisters held sister bertrille close
in the early seventies. sally field as flying nun
could do no wrong. when she took to sky, Almighty Jah
lifting palms to bring her near, frock as kite, flight
rebuking surf board. the vestal in 13D cups phone
with large hands, hands large enough for holy, belief

like my auntie, mama's third sister, who shares belief
and the flying nun's last name. pastor bonnell is closer
to the Prophet. her whisper fragile on the telephone
when we talk of mama. both labored for stiff anglican nuns
over thirty years at the hospital their nine children took flight
in a small town uncertain if black people could know Jah.

uncles, cousins and friends offer daily petitions to Jah
to climb inside aunties breaths, feed her good news and belief.
she is the last matriarch and we are selfish. please don't fly
from us, we pray. we want to shelter her, wrap her close
in cotton and light. weekday mornings they come, the nuns
who wash her body, chanting glory. on weekends they phone

hallelujahs. if i ask, will this saint three feet away send phone
mercies to my auntie? will frail pastor bonnell decipher Jah
in spanish? she's sending texts at 45,000 feet now, this rogue nun
who exorcises airplane procedure. the flight attendant believes
otherwise. his syrupy sweet requests fall mute as he bends close
yet again. his tongue is not sanctified. this anointed saint flies

heavenward hourly. only twice daily for the exasperated flight
attendant. who is the service provider for sister's cell phone
hotline to Jesus? five hours on southwest, embrace of sun close
and blinding. city of the angels not far. before every take-off i ask Jah
for traveling mercies, beg for a protective hedge in queasy belief
give thanks for safe journey. extra blessings to sit next to a nun.

15

a way of listening

for galway kinnell (1927-2014)

I.
after i received the letter a friend said
there would be culture shock. went
to bookstore instead. bought the gold
cell and blood, tin & straw, the book
of nightmares and one of your thirteen
new or selected or collected, many
with different versions of the same
poem. later in class you would poke
at yourself about this, that if it ain't
right fix it. it's yours. it will always
be yours to live with, like fergie's
delicate trod above the call of heavy
breathing and avenue c's ornette
coleman. nyc lacked jagged teeth
because you gave me compass
a bus token and spun me toward
sun, a boisterous light as charmed
as your wide smile and solemn grace.

II.
everyone tires. the body wearies.
shuts down briefly or more. here
we were, thirty graduate student
poets, maybe twenty-three. a few
hit the bar at sign of your droop.
some of us wondered how to feel
about your waking to an empty
room, if that might be frightening.

III.
tree frogs. you asked us to consider
the harmonics of south american
tree frogs in conversation. then
invoked a third language to engage
in the dialogue. others laughed.
some left. i heard wind & prayer & dirt
& the caution of elders in my skin.

IV.
after planes flew into buildings
you tried to help us find normal
all the while knowing there was
no such thing. we fussed about
you at the podium, cold towels
on forehead, hands to guide feet.
sharon in tears, stunned mute
the reading done before it was over.

descendent

i am holding my brothas hand
he walks ahead of me centuries

resist sixteen nineteen coffles
& whips in a sick society

resist eighteen thirty-three crackers
& furious dogs in a sick society

resist nineteen twenty-one noose
& mob in a sick society

resist nineteen fifty-five judge
& crow in a sick society

resist nineteen sixty-eight law
& order in a sick society

resist nineteen years of burge
& socket in a sick society

resist two-thousand thirteen cages
& apathy in a sick society

i am holding my sistas hand
she walks centuries ahead of me

all talk

for Chicago Public Radio's Every Other Hour series on Gun Violence

victim, a male black, 37, was involved in an argument

on an endless sidewalk where a child's pink four wheel brightens shadow
of tumblers on canvas of west side sky biting air an unexpected

august as helicopter hums it's blinking eye on 71st place.

this concrete outlines a-frames proud in their contrasting uniformity
quiet repose in the glare of a vigilant, almost open moon, peeking

between branches. both with secrets to share. fragmented truths
caged in police tape. few others are talking, yet the street is loud

and the front porch at this house pleads over the cacophony
of saturday night. a man, a son, a brother was shot on this stoop

mlk's determined face on the white front room wall questions
the two distinct marks in the door & the spotty wood outside.

red & pink flowers puzzle the round table beneath him, as he
wonders if the 1966 march brought us the freedom to live

where we choose, and covers his ears to the immediate pain:
bigots in virginia, cops talking irish bars & a black mama wailing

like a siren. the victim's sister is an angry parade
cops yell like she's a stranger on her own block. she curses

them & worries the street about the whereabouts of brother
& the adolescent boy who sought refuge just after bullets spoke.

this is an active crime scene she is told & denied entry to mama's
house. *just an altercation* they say. her tongue colors the neighbor's siding.

alley deep across the street, a crew of young men turn up
their volumes with tales of shootings & defying death

in ear shot of cops busy with routine distance

(elephants in the room)

A riot is the language of the unheard.
Reverend Dr. Martin Luther King, Jr.

I.

if a riot is the language of the unheard what
is silence? the disease of the privileged

the opioid of the wealthy or apathetic   silence
is only listening to the loudest mouth

an agreement from the ignorant legislation
of the partisan   silence is authorship

by the indifferent cries of the powerless & poor
is silence the echo of contrition drone & dirge

of the duped allegiance to the status quo
silence is sitting in a room when your boss

calls afrika & haiti *shithole countries*
& saying nothing silence is sitting

in a room to honor a native preacher
of a *shithole country* called atlanta

& speaking   still saying nothing

silence is seventeen in parkland fifty-eight
in vegas forty-nine in orlando twenty-six

in newtown six hundred & fifty in chicago
the nra cash in their accounts loud as an AR-15

II.

unarmed teachers revolt in red states teens
with machine gun vernacular spray

relentless hope angry tears blood
on their nikes they know testing

only assesses the number of prison beds
on the stock exchange at a school in a mexican

community a student wrote *he'd build
a wall around the hood to keep trump*

out as we worry the windows for tanks
militia or the ins our skin too anxious

for dreams   only white men can navigate
the world without code-switching

III.

i am not non-violent i am a teacher
i am not non-violent i am a writer

i am not non-violent i vote
we are not non-violent we care

walmart
republic
(2014)

bible belted: communion

did not know
black folks could be
catholic until i moved
to chicago. i was twenty-five.

bible belted: history

okie white men
are a curious herd.
never sure if cowboy
or cracker. skin coated
in dust from 1830 or 1921
hard to tell. they grow
whiter with age.

bible belted: good news

the evidence of things
not seen i believe. it's
what i have that is
unbelievable: trail of tears
revisited yearly, sam walton
worship. niggas the evil
root & cash crop.

bible belted: math

Pro-Black doesn't mean anti-anything.
El Hajj Malik El-Shabazz (Malcolm X)

there are at least twenty-seven
white people i love. i counted.

four from high school
five from undergraduate

years, maybe three from grad
school (one gay=bonus points)

and an assortment of compelling
melanin-deprived miscreants

in chicago and countrywide.
two brothas in the afterlife

remain why i add rather than
subtract.

the day russ died

after Frank O'hara

dark 4:30am sky buzzed alive
whatever birds sing that early
in brooklyn, discordant harmony
with clock nudge. hot water and towel

juice, vitamins, layers and coat, the corner
of east 46th street, dingy black town car
to utica. emerge forty minutes later from 4
train to odd still life. near campus, coffee

bagel, cinnamon-raisin from a bright
orange truck, long-haired bohemian
always chipper even in this frigid air
though manhattan knows little about winter.

steam from lips, students greet me in library
with poems, questions we mend. walk
to work at 10:30, the apple now spice
and sizzle. thursday, no class. 6 train to tribeca

hug sons at daycare, assemble
backpacks, outerwear. mama minutes later
in mini-van, angry streets, brooklyn
bridge, *which side to park today?* she wrestles

chicken, tofu, i splash naked boys, sculpt bubbles.
didn't hear it ring. when she calls me to dining room
sorrow is on our plates. hiking, he slid off table rock
dropped 85 feet, six waterfalls, body missing.

elegy

for Gwendolyn Brooks

I.

twelve years ago, met
chitown with $25, two suitcases
and a folder of poems, in search
of myself. you, haki and malcolm
had knocked enough red dirt
from my eyes to see black.

II.

i have seen your words
change rural fourth graders
into southside pool toughs,
hustling jazz in june.

III.

in class, you ignited riots,
watched us loot and ransack.

IV.

at dinner, your mortality
stiffened me, forced to consider
this in your absence, sobered
by the bone of your words.

altar call

I.

for brothas fathers husbands cousins
sons uncles nephews black manhood
in states of rebirth my teenage sons
groan to feet already half dreaming
food and football scores we stand
at rev's knees on red carpet at feet
of jesus beneath a twenty foot cross
with men we know and do not

scout leaders to the right (a confusion
i will never understand but have tried)
elders dressed sunday black men
carrying baby boys we place hands
on those by our sides bow

II.

i am at st.stephens a.m.e. swaddled
in thirty year old acned paneling
pews creak familiar mildewed
dustrag of flag between railing
and empty organ my cousins
near we are youth xmas show
easter pageant choir concert

i am looking for the church fan
family long to be flawless boy godly
teeth scripture by heart it never opens

III.

in a corner in a room
in a heart there is a door

through the door in a room
in a heart is a corner

turn the corner in a room
in the heart there is a door

through the door in a corner
there is a room in a heart

meet me there we will make
room in the corner for our hearts

IV.

i call them close wrap arms
around my selves share words
never uttered in childhood

after service we rouse youngest
winterize for city streets all hungry
and morning an anxious night

V.

attended church with daddy twice
both were funerals one was his

statement on the killing of patrick dorismond

a petty hoodlum (cop) shot/killed suspect (blackman) after hoodlum (pig) was told by suspect (haitian) that he (junglebunny) was not a drug dealer (nigga). the police commissioner (bounty hunter) referred to suspect (coon) as a "lowlife" (african) though his (aryan) comments were later proven false (white lies). the shooting (genocide) is the third (pattern) in thirteen months (institution) in which plain-clothes officers (gestapo) shot/killed an unarmed man (cheap blood). "I would urge (doubletalk) everyone (oprah) not to jump (dead nigga) to conclusions (acquittals)," mayor guiliani (watchdog) said, "and allow (blind faith) the facts (ethnic cleansing) to be analyzed (spin) and investigated (puppets) without people (darkies) trying to let their biases (racial profiling), their prejudices (welfare queen), their emotions (fuck tha police), their stereotypes (o.j.) dictate the results (status quo)."

klan march

perhaps in a sincere gesture of protest
the managing editor decided it best
i welcome the grand imperial wizard
to channel nine, guide him back to
the senior producer's glass cube
where he would proceed to engage
in heated words with the general
manager, whose robe hung upstairs
on the executive suite door. neither
of us offered our hands. staffers gathered
around me at the desk for a better view
of the meeting, questioned the cause
for vein pop and venom bleed
through office walls, summer sun
redefining our faces.

routine

every evening after the six o'clock
i ate dinner, something fast, sitting
at the desk. eight tv screens, three police
scanners talking to themselves
ears keen to chatter i'd not heard
earlier. check news radio at top of hour
just dry heat. then phones— seven p. m.
roll call—public information officers
at eight village precincts. *nothing*
goin on but a bunch of darkies drinkin
in del city. i am certain of his skin
secure inside the box, babylon's mouth
the lead story at ten, willie horton, sundowner
law still dripping. *you are talking to one.*
next day, managing editor assaults
his superior, attends while information
officer phones in apology.

rubble

for *Mrs. Clara Luper*

My biggest job now is making white people understand that black history is
white history. We cannot separate the two.
                        -Clara Luper, Associated Press interview, 2006

I.
dear mrs. luper

i knew you before that atlanta
preacher you were closer to home dirt
red from men sent to texas burdened
with mid june words fed a girlchild

in okfuskee county who understood jesus
was not inside a hospital that kept her sick
brother out the house near hammon
held together by a maid and brickworker

folk who ached their bones brittle
in august heat faith grown smile
a mask & truth *daddy said someday will be*
real soon tears long as endless walking

and as hope greenwood one hour
& three minutes on seventy-five fourteen
years of kingdom building ashes
in seventy two hours two years before love

& mercy birthed you here on this
god trembled land this almost native
this almost black this almost right
rooted in possibility and far-sighted

promise you put on those cat-eye
glasses to see yesterday today
and that a young child can lead
if she knows what is required

II.
twelve children three adults & you
at katz dressed in courage and spittle
the nation yawned okies awoke
six months and a year pre-greensboro

daddy never able to sit down and eat
a meal in a decent restaurant history
compels us to go let history alone
be our final judge state law upheld

your twenty six handcuffings twenty six
cellblocks twenty six steel wool blankets
twenty six concrete nights twenty six
are the children safe twenty six

i want to sleep in my bed

not everyone sat with you mrs. luper
legislated fear and lynching bees
men provide or don't john tubman
didn't think harriet was coming back either

like her, justice work and prayer filled your empty

III.
you said *if christianity fails* then *we surrender* perhaps it has
mrs.luper more likely we have stumbled on the path
still in rubble and debris we pray we are the center
you built with worn giving hands a slight remembering
of what was   a clear light on what remains to be done

sincerely

your son in progress

reluctant.

minivan

(2014)

a father's incantation

after Aracelis Girmay

here scraped knee and runny nose
here open eyes, laughter

here push swing, here
chicken nuggets, here soccer

ball, grace, here blue train
engine, backpack, summer

camp, swim trunks, here
what's for dinner? here what

are we doing today? here smelling
pee, testosterone, here books, science

counting to 100, ABC's, here gunshots
screams, short fuse, here prayer, here

prayer, here prayer, here a new day
cranky, hope, here respect, kindness

balance, here scabs, barber, tears, here
hugs, popsicles, here winter coat, the bill

is paid, here keep an eye on your brother
watch your mouth, here yes ma'am, call

your grandma, cha cha, rumba, jive, here
new shoes, clean clothes, here i don't wanna

take a bath, here strep throat, asthma, allergies
here more questions, answers daddy here

red eye

before sky has pondered mood
before sun knows right from left
before God, it is morning

and my little ones script a plan
for the day on pre-dawn darkness
with the light in their voices
and the night in my eyes.

when i find them the kitchen
is a train station, downtown
chicago the den, lake michigan
the bathroom sink. while mama

welcomes the gift of sleep and teen
sons hibernate in grumble, younger
brothers and me chart a course
on the newborn skin of saturday.

echolalia one

language echoing itself.
itself, echoing language
echoing language itself.
language, itself echoing

what i heard them say
say what? them, i heard.
heard them. what i say?
i say what them heard.

i mean these words
these words i mean.
mean these i words.
words mean: these, i.

why don't you hear me?
me you don't hear. why?
hear me, why don't you?
you don't? why? hear me.

you make me angry
angry you make me
make me angry: you
you angry. make me.

in my head i'm not alone.
alone, i'm not in my head.
head, i'm not in my alone
i'm in my head. not alone.

echolalia two

everyday he   reminds

how much more i need

        to learn

how smart i am

                not

how

      i think   i am

            smart

don't know

     sometimes

             if sad

is about

      missing mama

      or *franny's feet*

flight

I.
ari was in the backseat
of a squad car by the time
i arrived from class, tumblers
painting "the nine" midnight red, blue
red. annoyed butch sista next
door on my stoop, talking how she
could raise my son better, dcfs
already on way. rushing past
i thank her smugly, that she found
him wandering south on evans
mama's weary too deep. two
locks, two flights of stairs & two doors
then wildlife search for lost anaconda
diego and baby jaguar at his heels.
they knew something we lacked.

II.
tired daycare staff said anti-social
not behavior. he plays alone mostly
and enjoys hide and seek, the campus
labyrinth half a football field in size.
no one saw the buddyless boy join
a group walk down the long hall
past administrators and security.
out of door, handholders turn right
ari forward across drive, parking lot
his head lower than hood ornaments.
police spot him near cafeteria, a three
year old undergraduate darting back
to dorm for snack between class. they lose
him in square corridors, endless doors.
twenty minutes later i retrieve message
from office line, cell phone on file, on hip.

III.
gunfire and house arrest family
across street led us across town.
teen sons in age for *what you on*
nigga we found pacific heights in
chicago, playground down the block.
first weekend ari is nocturnal study
new quest, fresh terrain. we are
sprawling search party, hectic moonlight.
four lane, three blocks away, neighbor
spies him at intersection, calls police. bolts
and chains on doors next day too low.
fire escape invites back gate missing
two by four, alley eye open to last night's
corner.

trek

captain, i will go anywhere
you want to go, look both

ways before crossing galaxy
strange world where i lack

the vernacular, you fluent.
rouse me from carbon sleep

with details of mission, coordinates
lurking danger. i will be your

Q, number one, whoever
i must to enlist in this evolving

speculative fiction, magical realism
beyond human reach but not far.

earthlings so non-essential, feign
supremacy. outer space not final.

the spectrum

is a tenuous chaos
a bankrupt ritual
a tedious in-law
an irritable preoccupation
a vapid hoovermatic
a superpower
a kind of grace

golden

In life, there's the beginning and the end. The beginning don't matter. The end don't matter. All that matters is what you do in between – whether you're pre-pared to do what it takes to make change.

John Carlos, 1968 Olympic Bronze Medalist

not mexico city, sunny southside
afternoon. three hundred athletes in neon
tees at football stadium with no lights.

they approach the line, pause and release
softball. lands with pomp & plod, applause
tape measure and clipboard tally distance.

grass unaware of unimaginable feet
i sprint to hug my olympian, trudge
over, around competitors all buzzing

victors this bright and everyday.
ari mounts the podium like everest
giggles when his name is loud

lowers his head, red and blue ribbon
around his neck. gold, no mineral imbalance
here. then right arm, raised fist

in front of maple tree, god & creation
his impulse, unedited verse, truth
and the unexplainable joy in between.

conditioning

jumping jacks, deep bends, push-
ups, sit-ups, crab walk, 20-yard
dash, 50-yard sprint, five star, reverse
dash, shuttle run, rip drill, kickoffs
accelerators, butt kicks, high knee jumps
side jumps, cross steps, karaoke, 21-dive
37-toss, x-slant, hitting drills, y-fade, *how
ya feel? great! how ya feel? great!
who are we?* sweat, grit, struggle
water, choke, spit, pant, wind, heave
fight, whine, argue, question, repeat

uniform

this calm unnatural grass an order
a structure, a discipline out of place
in public ringed by chaotic brownstones
wailing streets. menchildren as soldiers.

i want to yell *hustle back, finish the drill.*
sun sheen on white helmets. for weeks
he waited for practice wear, sense of team
in fibers, logo. now i cannot find him.

space

couch again, elbowed
into a foot. four year

old grins in sleep.
i cannot, brown knit

fibers itch crusty knees.
msnbc sees me late

and early. teen sons
jabber fast as legs, the sun

an energy drink. juice
vitamins, coffee. breakfast

for two youngest— bananas
grapes, waffles, cereal. socks

shoes, coats, homework, clock.
beware the reluctant minivan

caged madness at 70 mph. blind-
side swerve, apologize by hand

lane too small for all of us.

male bonding

for Adrian, Christopher, Matthew, Greg, Roger, Major & Randall

i want my sons to know
men who smile

i want my sons to know men
who own their imperfections

i want my sons to know
men who listen

i want my sons to know
men who hear hearts, see words

i want my sons to know men
who honor women

i want my sons to know
men who appreciate the arts

i want my sons to know
men who adore their mamas

i want my sons to know men
who aren't afraid of tears

i want my sons to know
men who respect their fathers

i want my sons to know men
who use fists in self-defense only

i want my sons to know
men who value and dignify men

men who work hard, can't
spell quit, understand *no*

i want my sons to know
men who apologize

i want my sons to know men
who have relations with The Divine

men who question everything
men who know humility

i want my sons to know
men who read books

i want my sons to know men
who laugh at themselves

i want my sons to know
men who see possibility

richard pryor on the bicentennial

he stirred us crazy
(we were sure we were bad)
and replaced flip & red
for our juvenile impersonations

but when your parents
brought home that patriotic
record for your 12th birthday
they became crimson and you blue

in the afternoon secrecy
of your paneled bunker
richard taught class

we learned women in black
and white, american history in color

mr. oscar brown jr. goes to heaven

for Oscar Brown Jr. and Oscar "Bo" Brown III

I.
a jump and the buick spits a phlegmy tune
a pink-skirted sista asks *who got shot?*
youngbuck by the car is quick and numb
sirens wail black mama on my block

evans ave. begs & pleads for quiet
midnight sky grips a heavy truth
black people gather like some kind of riot
should be, but it's just spilled blood of youth

crackhouse two doors down is twenty-four seven
door knocking, wolf calling all night long
i kneel, pour libation to oscar in heaven
and wonder how would he tinder this song

from my front stoop (not my window) miles i see
roadmaps carved on stone black faces
the hardlust jones of living almost free
our hearts, our souls and other empty spaces

the air is dense with murder, lies & hate
blacks, lacking love, kill what looks like them
it's now memorial day, the sun is late
still the buick coughs up more phlegm

II.

i remember first your great bear hug
yes! you all are doin it! you said
after our set at some chicago club
bo thumpin bass til his digits bled

nate on tenor sax and doctor watts
keith & me with syllable and sound
lovely mama jean lovelied the spot
the funky wordsmyths were in the house

hard hittin black poetry in song
our mantra, our call to page & stage
your smile told us yes we did belong
go tell stories of black love and rage

III.

minister farrakhan, at your service,
said he did not know you but he knew
the rappers brought to the precipice
through stubborn earth you broke new

then the minister put out a call
for rap emcees to bring your words to life
afro blue instead of *kill them all*
signifying monkey's afterlife

mystic
turf
(2012)

african america

chunky girlchild swings
hips in street, a moving
traffic, body of drum
and horn. no crosswalk
to direct flow but contrapuntal
void a conversation
at gunpoint. transient script
a purposeful noise, food
for bootyshake. most don't
know the language. life
out loud.

city of bones

after August Wilson

in this town where no one wants to die
the crime rate is low everyone
clothed fed to belly full medicine
bountiful young people all
challenged to limit of potential a system
to support aptitude fresh air
& produce in our town women & girls
revered cherished protected men
gracious sensitive fitness prayer in multiple
tongue prison is those who do not
believe streets safe & clean a brotha
can get a cab free shuttle for the too high
in our town where no one wants
to die news always polite *the world played*
nice today...details at 10 no sickness starvation
lonely avoid walking on neighbors
lawn taxes paid on time haiti japan
spared all of us superheroes all of us
ordinary this town
not cairo madison tehran
no fly zone no gangs we assemble peace
gather in tiny or public space say excuse me
we are post race   no history beyond right
now maybe yesterday we can't remember

smolder

aunt 'ree has lived
through the mississippi
of sheeted heads
soiling family hands

she say
he got a white face
but he got blood
just like mine

she prays for better days
in the ashes of 1996
while a cross burns
the saints' meeting place

safe

he ate boogers and smelled like pee
the two scraggly goats looked inbred
as well   virgil's daddy the definition

of jiffy cornbread but too fucking mean
to keep weight   pitbull venom
every fourth word nasty and loud

as a monster truck   more afraid
of their house than his pops   nauseous carpet
cigarette wallpaper   a pasty white poverty

with bent hinges   virgil's mama
his father's sister   her fear gathered double
chins   i heard the beatings   three houses

down and across 10th   virgil curdling blood
out back   goats gnaw a baby doll leg
no school break   an ignorance bullies

found as duty   little sister screams like fists

blind

arnita was slow girth and mind   open window the call   train whistle
not my crowd knew who they were   where she lived   dirt road
wretch   poor house lean   which rich white boy   bait exchange
she gifted   snack packs   twinkies   in jeeps polo   cross border
eastside creep   your alone   head with no face   rode past once
drunk   late bloom   no stop   curtain trembles   night wind

braille

high on pcp, in-law beat sis until eyes
knotted. threw wall at my niece

then called daddy to boast handiwork
long distance murder threats

fifteen miles between them.
my sister's face raising

the mississippi in daddy's veins.
big sis and niece feel their way

through swollen night
drive into an elm tree, crawl

to the old pastor's door.
he was two counties gone

when paramedics offered reasons
to live, gave me reason to kill.

daddy's river a muddy bloodline.

crack house

greeter

she hustles us in
eyes tired

shadows stutter
behind nervous trees

outer room

screen door grime
a porous portal

paneling drips
frantic carpet

living room

up early ricki lake
an endless loop

tv's wide blue mouth
the only thing moving

pantry

she fast food she
buy one get one free

kitchen

parched bones
silently akimbo

peel of burn
gray of skin

he sizzles
cooks

mama sense: an elegy

scent

mama was loud, a live broadcast
the weather always spring

on her neck and bosom
she worked 3-11, so weekends

i watched her wrestle skirts over slips
long & white, check hose for runs

blouse and smock latched, the sugary
mist, flower water in angled ray and shadow

tiny shards rode parched afternoon
between tired beige curtains

touch

labor to find the words
an uneasy freedom jitters

of a woman whose core was salt
divine as laughter i spoke them

first new language to our dialect
twenty-four years lived in geography

and telephone wire changed little she
became awkward as adolescence

i was teenage smooth from town she
big-boned farm girl with smile vast

as texas *i love you mama* later
she let me hold her hand

sight

morning night finds me
in chatter with a flirting star

kiss skin of dream linger
as calm trees utter your name

it has not rained in days
bruised sun whispers storm to quiet

sound

my second son came quietly sixty
seconds before blue flushed red

has not stopped talking since his
tongue a net of lost time mama's

song only lessened the volume her tones
his colicky pillow rooted hum the balm

for a two-week bad day melody nothing
you know yet every cell swears it gospel

taste

after your mama dies
there is no guarantee
anyone will pray for you

wither

for Pops. for Mary.

1.

tuesday, storms uprooted her
fifty year old american elm.

eyes glassy ponds,
nervous throat. she knows

i 'm sad, but doesn't think
i care. trees are not worthy.

2.

two arteries drip on my father's brain
without tiring. surgeons suggest detours,

stomach reservoir. talk of shunts,
flow, distilling time.

3.

men bring machines,
resolve. leave a hole.

4.

her words on my shoulder
slouch like splintered limbs.

orphan

my dreams sleep in beds they have outgrown
nightmares leave room enough for any soul
i am the size of my own hollow promise
flush with life despite the darkening night

the preacher prays for me her vacant psalms
church fan perfect with a cutting smile
message unholy, steam rises from lips
why can't we speak the grace we all avoid?

might we choose a path the prophet walked?
mama knew the way to seek pure light
now i find me in her waning breath
wandering toward them with baby steps

i am anew, born in the pain of death
god forbid i lose all i have learned

eulogy two

we met on the first day of basketball practice at the armory. it was 1973. third grade. had round, short bodies; were forwards, you right of the paint, me left. we sucked. but made one another laugh and loved the game. we continued to be third string in almost every sport except the ability to laugh in the midst of madness. except life. twenty-seven years. you brought me bay city rollers and abba. i brought you earth, wind & fire. black boy and white boy in smalltown usa with an uneasy past. in 1975, my school closed due to desegregation. we became classmates. clowns competing for the highest gpa. i received the award for academic achievement, you the model student-citizen. so inseparable some thought us gay in junior high. was your high school cyrano. russ, you are my first love. you taught me courtesy and humility. i gave you freedom to be who you are, who you were.

halloween

when it was time for your dad's funeral
my folks brought me new shoes
flared jeans empty excuses

perched on the top stair
i screamed salty words

you didn't really forget
you just don't want me to go

white sneakers like rain

later i spoke with your mom
apologized for not being there
asked what could i do

she said be there so i was
at eight to sit with you
while jamie lee curtis

took our minds off death

eulogy three

should have never introduced you. blonde thin and fire. your type. my homegirl knew her. didn't see you again for a year and a half. had four classes together. fire resented our bond. denied access. saw you when banging head to concrete. worried about conception. when fire got too hot. the second time was freshman year of college, end of first semester. you were moving out to live with mike. snoring reminded you of deceased father, gone four years. i also refused to follow as did your new family, who were not new. girlfriend and two sidekicks, all holdovers from high school. hooked you up with girlfriend, whom i liked first. was over that. never close to tweedle-dee and dum. we were brothers. equals. you changed. came back upon meeting my new crew: punk rockers, artists, alternative think-ers. didn't leave again until falling in love with my ex (it occurs to me now we were an incestuous lot). moved out to be with her without me. never said why. found out in newspaper newsroom. tweedle-dee with you two, too. you abandoned me three times in twenty seven years. you always came back. come back now.

eulogy one

what was on your heart when the moss gave way. when you slid off that table rock. before the gorge snapped your back. before your body found the pool of the first waterfall, eight-five feet below. was it julie, who watched the soles of your boots vanish then held her breath thirty days until nature chose to share. or mama hutchison, chain smoking in the house on beverly she bought after your father passed. i pray it was grace. i yelped at the new york moon for you, brother. held vigil in union square whispering to smoke. nailed your image on trees. you came, finally, all calm and cold, with permission to write our handhold. corpus cristi or winston-salem. chicago or brooklyn. no matter. this will always be where we live.

eighth grade

I.

teens in kalamazoo tell me
words that spark indifference:
nigger (note spelling), bitch,
hoe (note spelling), then confirm
emcee's spat those lyrics at them
that week, that morning

II.

the n-word slouches with phonics:
er is insult, *a* is family. only
marshall mathers & other
bi-racial people can drop
nigga and not get beat down

III.

a nervous young man, who loves
rap, shows me his essay in confidence,
declines to read it to the class
they won't understand, they'll tease me
feels white boy is as bad as nigger
in the mouth of the beholder

IV.

it means *female dog* and since she is not
she can endure the gathering
of hooded nike super-heroes
who meet on fabulous corners
to consider every woman but her

she, herself also super, possesses
the ability to separate beat from lyric,
is certain fifty took all nine bullets,
of michael jackson's guilt, tupac's breath

73

public   school

runny nose   hormones
anxious reason   tense laughter
jigga what   man size
sagging light   vacant lot
long fuse   short trigger

dead dead

heat on the southside

I.

last night, police cordoned the four square
blocks surrounding my house in pursuit of a thug
who unloaded on the shell of a gangsta
in the funeral parlor filled with formaldehyde
and lead. black folks scattered, staining
complicated streets. i settle in for summer:
the maze to the front door, running teens
from my stoop smelling of weed and tragedy
reminding my sons they are not sources
of admiration, praying that might change. not yet
june heat rises like the murder rate, gleam
and pop already midnight's bitter tune.

II.

fifteen years ago, tyehimba jess
told me about a funeral home
with a drive through window.

you pull up, push a call button
through bulletproof glass a friendly
somber attendant takes your request.

moments later, casket open
your order appears for review.

at the time i thought it inhumane.
now i think about the abstraction
of friendship while counting bullets.

III.

is there an extra dead?
what is the term for dying again
when already? killing chi?

and what of the corpses that walk
my block in the anonymity
of black skin and white tees
filled with fluid?

body shop

i've heard tell of a hustle
in brooklyn where clever folks
throw themselves in front of cars
lurching down eastern parkway.

not the beat-up green mini-vans
or duct tape toyotas of poets, not
impalas bleeding chrome
spinning disposable testosterone.

but mid to high end machines
of certain insurance booty, drivers
in the 30 to 50 year range, same
demographic as oprah's audience.

i suppose there is a right and wrong
approach to this science, the angles
of minimal damage to consider, side
to bumper, back to door, head up

unless her poodle is well groomed.
few have retired, i would speculate
but work less now that checks
lack bounce and the mailman walks briskly.

it must be the eyes, wide and clean
that distinguish these impact alvin aileys
from ordinary jaywalkers.

at utica i marvel at the desperate genius
the split-second calculus, the risks and gains
of such occupation, before descent
into the dark anonymity of the 4 train

crutch

when i was younger
most of the men i knew

couldn't stand up straight
couldn't bend their knees

they struggled to walk
gravity against them

in my teens
it was cool to pimp

one leg with purpose
the other wandered lazily

now young men move
swiftly one leg with purpose

the other stiff and loaded
i am older   my limbs remember

uncle lawrence's canes
rest at the bottom of the stairs

bloodsoil
(2009)

mascot

for zack. for mark.

I.

the red undertones that inform my melanin
were birthed in the black mountain foothills
near the tennessee-mississippi border.

my great grandfather albert found freedom
just before the trail of tears migration
and hooked up with an ornery black
woman in westpoint, muddy waters' neighbor.

ms. cora mae, never one to hold anything
long but money, sent him to his horse
upon the news—she had things to do—my grandma
would join the family business in a while.

ms. cora mae carried three daughters and two sons
into post-reconstruction mississippi, sown
from different seeds. the women, their doors
always open, were sexy to kill for. the men
loyal enough to do the job—cooking shine and running
game.
      when the klan came calling the guns were loaded.
my father and uncles, all under ms. cora mae's command
led rebellion against attack on their cottage industry, left
red cotton to feed brittle soil, then scattered in four directions.

after three draft dodging years in miami, daddy ended
up in oklahoma, where his sisters somehow landed
and his mama joined them after california.

II.

i am an okie. grew up on cherokee
as did zack, my first best friend,
who lived two blocks away and wore
the street in his skin. we liked basketball,
cars, and never watched westerns.
zack disappeared in high school after one year
in warpaint riding a spotted mare at pre-game.
he was gone before i had the chance
to tell him what i already knew.

grandma never claimed native and hated
anyone darker than a grocery bag. this is where
i begin, on cherokee, trying to find zack
to talk about this mascot issue.

III.

the beantown honkies
the johnson city jarheads
the washington senators
the oaktown wannabees
the cushing crackers
the tulsa rednecks
the old baltimore bigots
the chicago police department
the white city afrikaaners
the cook county overseers
the heritage foundation
the riverside peckerwoods
the german shepherds

IV.

How politically correct can we get? To me, the folks who make these decisions need to get out more often. I think they insult those people by telling them, 'No. No. You're not smart enough to understand this. You should be feeling really horrible about it.' It's ridiculous.
    Jeb Bush, Governor of Florida *

*St. Petersburg (Fla.) Times, August 10, 2005

V.

ms. brooks urged me to return to school
from the nervous backseat of my mustang
in 1994. but what triggered the movement
was an enid, oklahoma drunken conversation
in a honky tonk with friends from high school,
all white and pseudo-liberal. we deliberated
level playing fields & jesse jackson
while the sad child of hank williams warbled
something loud about loneliness. just as twelve
years prior, i was cultural diversity at the table
and no longer comfortable. one man, maybe
my closest oklahomey in the bar, assured me
the residuals of chattel slavery no longer existed,
while leaning against the door of a 100-year-old
family business. i enrolled in african american
studies two months later. he will not remember
this exchange any more than he will recall the night
i was informed my blackness was a liability
in his pursuit of teenage pussy. history will tell on you.

cleaning graves in calvert

for Papa Johnny Hodge, my Great-Great Grandfather

under a crying elder willow
we meet the 107 degree shade
bearing thirsty earth
from which i sprang

a safehouse next door to
a tinderbox church
sanctuary from hot

lone star nights.
though your face is hidden
i feel you in the folds

calling beyond the tired summer
crops to bring us here

we were last to know
ritual precedes emancipation

haunted

for Agha Shahid Ali

on a train reading shahid's poems
about his mother's death thinking of mine

at a festival in virginia he crowned me
ali #2, then flirted relentlessly

in indiana, where radio is a lonely
place, i linger on our mothers, shahid

and how home is not when mama's gone
spit of smoke and powerlines ornate

birdless dusk, the burnt tar odor of gasping
midwestern ideas. even football field lights

dim this friday. brother this is my birthplace
born like this with dirt in my hair

if we were lovers we'd visit oklahoma
my father loathing your manliness

mama admiring your soap opera vocabulary
my parents are gone, shahid, as are you and yours

*Thus I swear, here and now, not to forgive the universe
that would let me get used to a universe*

without you...

nature

wichita mountains, medicine park, ok

we hiked over an hour
cockleburs question our ankles

sweat bleeds dry sun
tears our somber ascent

summit elbows cloud
gorge a wide red grin

river drools miles below

tod unwrapped the plastic
around you   kissed god

gave half of you back
then handed me the urn

i guided you to sky
you refused to leave

grit of you in my mouth

harvest

yellow-gold overgrowth

wheat like children raising
arms high to be picked. everywhere
is shaft scraping cloud, every
where is nowhere, what's behind
looks like what's ahead.

a boy no more than twelve
commanding earth, tiny monarch
in green glass, a southwestern
pope-mobile sweating progress.

the smooth hand of machine.

after harvest

from mullet to buzz cut

used up breadbasket for a world
that barely cares, tips cereal
box. braided rows half unkempt, tossed
by god's breathing. jagged stubble
in blistering sun, the almost

bald head endless flat. mane cropped
by fortress that blocks traffic in both
directions. vaulted cockpit a telephone
booth with hips, helix of blade a sinister grin.

idle, only sky to fill time.

blur

sulking two lane highway
herefords and steer wave
sad, watery eyes, mouth
mouthfuls of bad manners.

this mid-sized sportscar
momentary thrill, quick
escape from mulch, ominous
future. a crimson valley

just beyond the fading idea
of intersection, karen silkwood's pale
imprint—lifeless silos, limping
tallgrass. a town named crescent

struggling to recover after death
her murder wrought three decades
gone. speed zone—55, 45, then 35
now 25, pentecostal church, bowing

a-frames, tasty treet, jail, post
office, then 35, 45, 55, 70—a memory
withering on the roadside.

anadarko blue

sunday hung out by the corner
with nowhere to go

without concern
for changing events

or turning stomachs
brotha's huddling in a parking lot

passing a spliff
and eating church's chicken

you weren't home

playing hooky

for jimbo

sitting here with you watching
middle america gnaw on itself

newlyweds roll their newborn
past a silver speedboat

its sleek design, promise of adventure
a cadence that sways listless pines

running in place

my six month old son
is snoring. at 2:30 a.m.
this breath brings memory:
the must of hangover
while television watches daddy
sleep off another two-day retreat.
the cowboys-eagles game unfolds.

upright by the easy chair,
his boots taunt me.
the muddy cowhide murmur
tales of red clay & big sky
only to find themselves here.
their point is mockery;
such confidence of direction,

purpose. here, alone
with these menacing boots,
their fresh dirt and daddy's
snoring. at 2:37 a.m.
my son changes position.

sunday at mutha's

Boy, don't you kick that ball in tha garden. If you kick that
ball in tha garden one mo time, imma tan yo' little brown hiney!
                    Anna "Mutha" Lawrence

we could hardly wait for crusty ol' reverend
jenkins' final *amen* so the real sunday
afternoon could commence.

fried chicken and fresh catfish.
aunt maudell's potato salad.
aunt bonnell's sweet sweetcakes.

fresh corn on the cob and green
beans from mutha's garden.

more than a plot of plowed soil, this was
community center, where her children worked
sad earth, where her grandkids destroyed it fifty yards away.

she sat on the sagging porch, lifted
by four high cinder blocks, to watch the sabbath unfold.

almost unholy how worship affects
young black appetites but my cousins and me
were squirming in choir pews for one reason:

kickball. no game ever completed. always
some form of tragedy--pam skinning up her knee,
chucky throwing the ball hard upside rae's head

or losing skipper to the kitchen. he ate
everything. all the time. once he made a salad
dressing sandwich on white bread.

man, that's some nasty stuff.

another time in the kitchen two nieces
and a nephew were covered from head
to toe in chocolate. it was ex-lax.

fear entering mutha's bathroom.
sometimes the light chain stuck.
pulling, trying to hit the stool, you knew a whuppin' was coming
if you missed. an old maple traced the window.

the inside of your pants warm and sticky.

when mutha joined the ancestors
jaybird moved into her house
front porch supported by the same
cement squares. it didn't feel right.
but i wasn't afraid to use the toilet.

on the day of the harmonic convergence

a 1972 audi fox (known as
the sun car because my homeys
cut out most of the roof and its hue)
which had sat idle for eight months
started without a second thought

it was elvis' birthday

and though we knew this we didn't realize
until we drove to the store (in russ' ride--
the sun car set half a block earlier)
to learn royalty was in the park

all the planets aligned

it was not our fault they became angry at us
laughing at the poor excuse for a dead king
jiggling pasty flesh in august heat

it was not coincidence

we went back to the purple basement
built a shrine to capture music
between us felt earth push and spin

give and go

this united center
was outside, my backdoor
backyard arena packed
sundays sweaty. swearing

jabbar stood closer to god
than moses, i witnessed
gravity turned sideways
by high school brotha's

in knee high tube socks.
i collected their moves
like germs on a six year old:
lacey's shake and bake,

clifford's turnaround in-yo-face,
dewayne's deadly twenty-footer, and
crazy cousin larry's baby
sky hook, which could never be

released without calling his name:
*uh-oh, it's kareem abdul-jabbar
with the unstoppable hook shot!,*
larry would scream, one thirteen inch

foot over my head. the big boys
let me hang because of dede,
my sister, who they all liked.
besides, it was my yard and

my goal. even though larry
nailed the hoop too high
on the backboard, i learned
to play big with my squat body,

and grew to appreciate the metaphor.

sport

I.

this photographer's weekly work is peddling
virility: soft porn by day, pro ball nights
and weekends. eyes itchy from the substance
of dreams he slumps into a glass of vodka

there are no flaws in fantasy

then slurs colleagues follow barack's every
move. i have seen them, south lake
shore drive a parting water at dusk—
six motorcycles, three homeland security
impalas, white and blue, two khaki mini-
buses, four limos, smoke. barrels aimed
cellulose snap and burn, a neck in a rag top.

II.

populism is pejorative: one man's
community is another's advancing
army. niggas of mass destruction.
so what do we do with this?

III.

said one of his buddies shot two
frames all day. *why waste film?*

IV.

i am sooner red, a native of the most
right state in the confederation. shamefully
almost as geeked my school will vie for the title
as i am barack gracefully corrected pundits. the bcs
is like benefiting from a bad call. this time sooners
found good fortune and a heisman. in a moment
of deep tragedy i revisited my freshman yearbook:
switzer's eroding might, wayman tisdale and marcus
dupree. old new faces, my two best friends alive. on
fraternity row, halloween 1982, white boy as kkk, as
west african, as uncle ben. 1976 the last year sun
didn't set on blacks in norman. think of all the games
won by then.

V.

spent the entire campaign deflecting this mad
prophecy more probable than fiction. the country
suffers from narcolepsy and gout, with side
effects from the medicine. they are growing
in number. so are we. they all look alike.
we do not. they comfort in closed hands.
ours are open and many. get that picture.

pilgrimage

body africa is almost sick almost
healthy thin about the waist bone
weak to bone belligerent joints
frantic memory perpetual fever

and again the desert's toothless mouth
as weathered palm rouge to solemn
bronze *nothing is moving* she whispers
only sand that bears your name

the mediterranean makes its point: i am not
where you are algeria's glassy forehead
to furrowed brow the sahara's hot breath
incessant stutter dusky cough of cloud

older here sun wrinkles
toward ocean weary of moon
i long to kiss the endless
horizon   the sediment of our sons

ankle high in questions

they shall run:

harriet tubman poems (2004)

harriet

truth

massus metal weight
push in ma headbone

i was round thirteen
den dem say i'se dull

now i know de lord
hear me in prayer

much mo like talk tho
we's all de time talkin

when i wash my face
i says lord make me clean

when i take up de broom
lord sweep sin from my heart

when i took dat blow on de head
i pray dat chile knows free

when de blackness come
i go where God want

harriet

spark

henry & charles come again
last night wid mo papers
bout turner cross de bay

in de cabin flickerlight
we huddle quiet as sleep
henry read like soft wind

say nat done killed a mess
of white folks dey still
can't trap him dogs nosin

all ova de hills been weeks
now some white folks fraid
dem say we a hornet's nest

some wanna set us free say it
ain't right we on de winepress
de south ridin our backsides

dey'd all like ta hold turner
say he got faith like fever
holy ghost shakin his belly

harriet

lightning

second time befo sunday
charles & henry stoop here
faces bent wid gray sky

mush and bacon clean gone
dey tell how white troops
shoot and shoot and shoot

say dem kill evryting negro
round de bay dem snatch
nat cage him til de gallows

loosed his spirit heaven boun
de yoke christ borne laid down
fireblood comin i shut my eyes

see jesus on de rugged cross
snakes slickin bout de ground
sun lazy hind de moon

harriet

long way home

john lord knows you still vexed   reckon me too if my wife stole
off durin sleepy night god an de devil only souls up at dat hour
even if i knows she bout to be sold south   even if i knows she
was leevin an you did   you so troubled when i talk bout leevin
call me a fool call me cudjo five years wid you john   yo wife
bout to be sold away jus cus you free dis don't worry you none
you laugh   dunno if i'd miss yo laugh if i was in de south tho
thank ya jesus gotta room in phildelphia john   aint big but clean
nuf room fo us some chirren too yo baby   i aint too old jus yet
jus round thirty-one i think   make us a home john   one
where we's both free free from de lash's shadow free like de lord
mean   got dis suit fo ya john   aint nobody worn dese clothes befo
walk proud in dese clothes dese is free mans clothes

john tubman

faithless

I would have freed thousands mo,
If dey had known dey were slaves.
                    --Harriet

herd on da wind you come back fo me
didn't think you come back fo me
didn't think you come back at all
been so long my skin grew tired

dis life too hard to know all alone
caroline cover me jus fine
she a quilt ginst da cold in ma blood
she mend de torn spots in ma soul

aint got no mind ta leev dis place
go on moses find yo promise lan
mines is here beside dis fire
wid folks we knows from when we's born

harriet

hole

dis suit of clothes jus as empty
as a sky wid no stars
two years a workin savin money
den   john drop out my heart

i dont want ta see his wife
i knows dat she is me
i'se could go in   shootin de rifle
let my angry run free

bes not   jus my temper risin
no use stokin dead fire
but ta see his face one mo time
now lord   jus you on high

if he make do widout me now
i can make do lord i can make do

isaiah

the leaving

my lord she gone
again we's in de middle
of pitch black sky

moon see us only
we pray starin back
from de murky river

thirteen of us i think
nigga runaways crossin
wide water wid no ripple

all cold an shiver
she gone again my lord
why here aint de red sea

where she go when she go

harriet

burdens

folk live in ma bones
breathe ma breath
we night like skin

i bear de weight
ma back bent ta light

draggin de moon
like a shackle

i pray dis night
is silent as dawn's feet

harriet

paregoric

shush now chile
dis stuff keep you down
for a while   dat other
stuff keep you down
a while longer

harriet

fodderhouse

dis mornin milk of sun
seep through de lookhole

devils crouchin
on de walls udda side

night is busy worrisome
day a tirin idle

lord hide de outcast
betray him not dat wander

six chirren five women
seven grown menfolk

saints grievin today
dey trampled yesterday

run chirren run wid yo grief til it heal
cry out til you ride above tears

negro hunter

headprice

this nigger too damn dumb to know how much
he's worth. those woods by the thompson place
must be filled with hunters tracking this joe.
first a thousand, then fifteen hundred,
now two thousand. "all expenses clear and clean
for his body in the easton jail." sue worrying me
to settle down with another kid coming.
aching hard to get out her mama's house.
how she think i'm make that happen?
ain't got much, don't own no land.
had to borrow this pack of bloodhounds.
six cents a mile, two dollars a day. this pack
smell em a mile off. smart. mean too.
seen em tree a nigger, pull him out a gully,
gnaw him to bleeding, every penny well spent.

negro dog

thoughts on the matter of runaways

don't mind showin my teeth
means i get to work
my legs and savor that hunk of meat
after i track em down

don't even see a coon
unless i'm trainin or chasin
master stick an old shirt or scrap
under my snout and i'm gone

he doesn't let me out
for anythin else   i live to run
this cage makes me crazy
leaves my blood funny

coons really aren't hard ta catch
they have to sleep sometime

the parable of jacob

once upon time there was a young enslaved african named jacob
who lived in baltimore county, maryland on the plantation of a mister
crockett (not the nicest man in the world) one evening after working in
the field for fourteen hours in the july heat and being forced to witness
the lashing of his best friend jacob decided it was time to leave he
fed and watered the dogs as usual rubbed their bellies one by one and
hummed his goodnight tune then went to his cabin to eat dinner he
laid on his quilt and thought about which route to take on his escape
he tried to rest but was too anxious to sleep finally the still of night
arrived jacob peeked out of his cabin door located the north star crept
through the slave quarters and slipped quietly into the meeting of trees
just northwest of the plantation he ran for what felt like days tired and
out of breath he crouched under the dense of a juniper tree where dawn
found him startled by the sun and a strange smell jacob awoke to the
sweaty liquored scent of massa henson the overseer from the covey
place drunk and looking for a spot to piss on his way to work henson
stumbled right into jacob's hiding place now henson's rifle was pointed
at his head he stood jacob up put his arms and legs in coffles chained
him to the back of his wagon and dragged him the thirty miles back
home massa crockett gave henson twenty-five dollars called his overseer
and together tied jacob's arms and legs to a tall elm crockett took out a
blade and began to cut at jacob's limbs when he spoke *i knows you like
to hunt massa you a good shot why dontcha get de gun untie me and give
me fifty paces?* crockett liked this idea and sent the overseer to load two
rifles guns in hand the two men untied jacob and watched him scamper
into the forest crockett commanded the dogs to make chase they didn't
move he called them again to run still they wouldn't budge frustrated
crockett ran to the dogs and screamed while his overseer mounted a
horse to track jacob the overseer never found him the dogs never moved

seven months

ghost of hold
fist of ache

fever of spit
must of prey

gut of tear
lash of sweat

want of dirt

flesh
wind

lurch of crow
talk of leaf

curse of bark
tomb of blood

hollow of tree
tight belly of moon

harriet

fate

coldhot snakes ma skin
thundercloud starts ma head
dis feverbed deep water

breath weak an bone sore
lord canada aint seen me
de men still up north john

ya name me general our plan
aint no good ta ya in new york
ma heart dere in virginia

gideons sword in yo hand now
holy soldiers lambs blood clean
holy soldiers negro an white

strike make sweet yo days

harriet

aftermath

sanborn say five negro men an sixteen
white men walk ta de throne
at harpers ferry   he say dey hold

de town an de guns an de bridges
fo a time den troops kill evrybody
dem hang john from de pole

fireblood comin ma eyes river
see gates swung wide old man
lay down yo angry john brown rest

jacob jackson

christmas presents: code

ol postmassa floyd sent rufus
to tell me come get dis letter
(truth i have never liked rufus
but there aren't many white folk to like
i don't have to like them now just
stay out their way and mind my keep)

i walks after rufus   his mare
trot slow de road a muddy slop
de oak trees shakin winter stiff
when we get inside postmassa's
floyd and capn smith dey vexin
ovuh dis here paper sent me

i took it up'n read tha thing
twas from william henry ma boy
up north in one a dem free states
(i know why capn and floyd vexed
this letter might be from the devil
himself from way they're looking at me)
seem like a fine letter til dis:

read my letter to the old folks
and give my love to them and tell
my brothers to be always
watching unto prayer and when
the good old ship of zion comes
along to be ready to step
on board --signed william henry jackson

i read it ovuh and ovuh
i said aloud:

> "dat letter can't be sent for me
> i'se can't make head no tail of it"

i hands it ta floyd den walk out
(she's coming to fetch her kinfolk)
headin east for home coondog quick
send sarah to de thompson place

116

lil john ross

christmas presents: heir

daddy
left home

two hours
after i came

know
his heartbeat

don't know

his face
taste

fear in
mama's milk

all day
sour

migration song

ma sista lutie boun ta go
hope ta meet ya in heaven
ma brotha william boun ta go
hope ta meet ya in heaven

ma uncle johnny boun ta go
hope ta meet ya in heaven
ma auntie ruby boun ta go
i hopes ta meet ya in heaven

jesus stoop down
an wore a man's life
he died a man's death
ta free our strife

ma granny addie bell boun ta go
hope ta meet ya in heaven
ma grandpa cogman boun ta go
i hopes ta meet ya in heaven

ma mother ol' rit boun ta go
hope ta meet ya in heaven
know my ol' soul boun ta go
i hopes ta meet ya in heaven

southside rain
(2000)

learning to swim

for a teacher in need of permanent vacation

his sleeves rolled up tight revealing veins popping
blood pressure rising like his voice like the sound
of a broken yardstick slammed against a desk
where questioning hormones reflect
the tension of yesterday's drive-by
the glass shattered in rage from slamming the door
too hard to not notice the sweat veiling red eyes
the tears escaping quietly to the floor
where one bright-eyed fourth grader gasps for air

she knows the right answer

she is drowning

breathing room

teachers lounge
in the tiny space
between math and microwave.

we speak of Jesus
and All My Children
with equal compassion.

a small black and white
battles the static.
its foil antenna
receives mixed messages.

a half empty vending machine
squats impatiently in the corner.

but the bell chimes its piper's song
urging us reluctantly
toward the future.

southside rain

southside rain visits darkened corridors
falls through cracks where children dream
falls through cracks of textbook lies
and dampens hungry minds

southside rain collects in poison puddles
on playgrounds of potholed wishes
these schools are just treading water
and washing belly empty upon the pavement

we've brought the sky down on us
we've brought the sky
acid rain flows through my veins
some wonder why
(and the rain keeps falling)

southside rain seeps through unstable foundations
divides where there's no shelter
conquers where there's no hope
and mildews the rotting floor

southside rain is tears on the angel's face
searching for a place to rest
waiting for a time of truth
so her moans can cease

southside rain drops like false prophets
southside rain drops like my brother's blood
southside rain drops like our leaders
southside rain drops like my knees

our sons

for the seven and eight year old boys wrongly accused
in the murder of eleven year old ryan harris

the difference between
the truth and a lie

separates a one inch skull
fracture and a rock
chucked by a seven-year old.

blue beads grip
his braids, jerking
as he nods in response.

if he grows up
he hopes to join
chicago's finest gang.

they drive fast cars,
carry big guns,
always live on tv.

just a few more questions, ma'am.

the wooden bench
no more comfortable
than it has ever been.

in chicago, justice is
a room with no windows.

her boy, seven, is hungry,
confused. she can feel it
from the muffled hallway

door cracked. dark
as frantic shadows.
daddy is not allowed

to enter the station
guards hold back
fire. the englewood moon
a pale, knowing bulb.

the boys, low-rent refugees
from third world corners,
bend, then break: confess

over happy
meals. they will be
forgotten like quiet bicycles.

tracks

scene at 71st and dorchester

pretty as a picture this
image faded at the corners
sepia four-chord tones
circa 1930, only it's nineteen-ninety
now howling winds moan
a dusty, pregnant sorrow
at that place where tracks
meet hard black road
way off on the otherside of last night
when he spun like an empty bottle and
sought somewhere else to lay his hat
down the line, the whistle blows knowingly
her companion rests at her feet
brittle, worn from walking
they pause between rails
stretching endlessly southward
to disappear with the sobering sun.

the dog looking for his best friend.
the sista looking for her dog.

six strings strum a sad sermon.

sixty-third & cottage grove

a new abandoned canopy promises
ghost train rides while providing refuge
from the backstabbing moonlight

twenty-four hour corner summit
meeting midnight minds inside workshirts
stained beyond weary demands for attention

greasy spoons fall by the northside
neon flickering convenience and no surprise
amidst the despair are smiles
true enough to call home

working women wait on tips gracefully
side-stepping after dinner invitations
heads held high, serving retort

salmon patties pepper p.m. hunger pangs
addressing eggs scrambled beyond indifference
as is our waitress, with too many tables

crescent, ok.

the true sense of humankind's will
to live
is based upon grey days
and early december chill.
when stagnant pools
staid collections
and last week's tears
evolve from slouching drizzle.

skies of sunday's melancholia
highway seventy-four south.
quilted patches of green
brown
red
weave the horizon
in a cyclical blaze
of rusting ingenuity.

lonely intersections spontaneously pocket
elusive moments of congregation.

standing still
is a tempo.

woolworth's poem

for russ and tod

I.
we rode summer on ten speeds
bike routes to the courthouse lawn
where parking meter hitching posts
lined melting, technicolor days.

II.
we knew every corner
from the bird droppings in the basement
to the scent of musty popcorn.

III.
we laughed in the face of history.
him, golden locked and chubby nosed.
me, bubbling hot fudge.
we dared lunch counters innocently.
so close some thought us lovers.
we were.

IV.
the parakeets and canaries are no more.
silence creeps the arthritic escalator.
those fat, paisty, sandwich fingers
labor now in snaptight kitchens
across town, their tenderness lost.

V.
tod gave me a coffee mug
on the last day of business
before it became a museum.
he sat where freedom's students
wore ketchup and abuse
in a pre-jordan north carolina.
it is a simple mug.
opaque, speckled clay.
rounded handle.
sides geometrically balanced. sturdy.
it meant a lot to him
to give it to me.
it meant a lot to me to have it

homemade

i was made in st. stephens church
on choir pews behind an ageless pulpit.
under the almighty eye of mutha,
my cousins and i, led by aunties,
crafted stodgy hymns into poetry
with the love of God and song.

al green coloured saturday's song,
but flickering spirits painted church
sundays in deep human poetry.
our voices reached the oak pulpit,
then the small congregation, while aunties
bonnell and maudell stirred mutha

to rock and hum their gentle music. mutha
raised seven children on gospel song
and hard work. my mama, two uncles, & four aunties
talked with God in a tiny texas church
where an easy-tongued preacher stroked the pulpit,
sharing scripture as hereditary poetry.

between prayers they tilled poetry
with blood and sweat. in the garden, mutha
produced converts from her earthen pulpit:
stubborn tomatoes. melons ripe with tender song.
praising the hallowed floor of this church,
this land that knows my uncles and aunties

by name. led by my soulful aunties,
the family left calvert, texas, to inspire poetry
a little further north. they found a church
home in a place called enid, then sent for mutha.
this tired soil, this birthplace of mama's song
was now a fond remembering, a lonely pulpit.

the space between preacher and pulpit
remains sacred. one of my aunties
now resides there, naturally. her song
full of light. her love like the poetry
of my sons' laughter. i feel mutha
everywhere. i know she's always church.

kneeling at church, i consider the pulpit,
dream about mutha and cherish my aunties
a narrow rift divides poetry and song.

patchwork

we have abandoned our loom.
no strings attached.
tapestry weakened by worldly strain.
torn this way and that.
led by the infectious tug
which splits the difference
we make when we are whole.
not fringes in the fabric.
when rifts are deep
hands can grow idle.

i look at my hands.
i see from miles and myles.
these appendages have lived four thousand lives
have raised the earth from kenya to kentucky
have defended both projects and pyramids
have touched the lifeforce of passing spirits, and
in an effort to find a solid grasp
have ripped the tapestry.

my sistas clutch forgotten rainbows.
more of my brothas holding black steel.
do we continue to tear the fabric
or with umoja
piece the fragments together.

our loom us Mama Afrika.
our loom is her scattered watoto.
our loom is in our hands.

cockroach
children
(1995)

passage

I.
sirens scream another nighttime episode
as beads of moisture cling
to telephone wires, they shimmer
a glittery dance to pulsing red and blue
illuminescence
tired steps, familiar tunes
like the busstop turned electric slide
city rhythms a sad repetition
reborn at every sunset

II.
six young bloods inhabit the corner
of Division and Green
we reek in concrete colors
and smell
full of bull
or so read the epitaphs
on the forty ounce tombstones
at our feet

these city nomads adjust heavy burdens
to balance against the oncoming night
a nocturnal reoccurrence
waitin' on the bus
waitin' on the hands to move
waitin' on change
waitin' on justice
waitin' on tomorrow
silently prayin' for warmer days

we speak of conquest
as the sky sings of broken dreams
and dead bodies
we check our manhood momentarily
as the westbound bus lurches into darkness,
we stand as five

the lure of phat beats
and gyrating hips
send two brotha's away
pushin' kicks on pavement

after a collective pocket dig
two strike enough gold
for another malt liquor ride
the bright lights leadin' them on

alone
one discovers pen and paper
and tries to hide
behind his words

all of us gone
in search of our fathers
in different direction

still life

pain wore her face
like a road map...

travelling thru years and tears
to a moment which ceases to leave.
And what could he do?
what's a boy to do
with the weight of the worlds
while he's still nursing?
thirty-seven years
is too long
to be on the bottle.
once, he day-dreamed of flight
she would sit beside him,
they would sit together.
now, punch-drunk
and
feet failing,
he is hopelessly
grounded.

she cannot be found.
she's out looking for him.
you kkkeep your damn hands
offa me!
she finds him.
nogoodsorryassednigga!
she finds him in the face
of every startled stranger.
don't you hit me again!
stop following me!
she finds him at every corner
while traveling thru years and tears
to a moment which ceases to leave.

71st & king

night smells catfish crispness
while sista-girl works them curls
S's Lounge buzz and slams
buzz and slams
buzz and slams
as brothas basehead
brothas boomin
bass
head brothas boomin
base boomin
boomin bass
blowing the plastic in the used-to-be back window
a baby boppin in the backseat
jackie's restaurant is always open...
until 11:30pm
urban queens with newport lips
hardened softness serving biscuits of like texture
leo's flowers a fading pastel
succumbs to evening wings·
chicken wings
wild irish the bouquet of the hood

rogers park

at times like now
when words seem a chore
and 71st Street a city away
images roll by yawning September
days dancing against lakeside dusk
poetry is hard to find here
save the wizened oak
crying seasonal tears
ambivalent leaves ride the air
the avenue a sea of autumn
i rake the words into piles
and dive into an elusive blanket

window

(a peace offering)

yesterday holds no promise
other than learning for today
things may look the same
outside the window/frame
but, wind has rustled the branches
leaves have abandoned our familiar
colours fade to winter pale

peering out, I often see tomorrow
bundled up warm and tight
holding her mother's hand
she checks both ways
before crossing the street
the crunchy beneath her feet
she imagines walking on the moon

unlike television,
this glass box captures present moments
fleeting seconds reflective in scope
because we will never be here again
like memory free from hindsight...
the pane is in need to repair
there's much work to be done

these words may not be worth
the paper on which they're written
they may not be worth the chasm
that denies our dread lock
but, they represent vision to me
hand extended
window open

Acknowledgements

Thanks to Shawn Crawford, The Calliope Group LLC , Lindsey Smith and the mighty Tri-City Collective (Najah Hylton, Bracken Klar and Joshua Wann) for creating a world of change in a world in need of change.

Special thanks to Third World Press, Willow Books, Living Arts Press, Voices from the American Land, and Mongrel Empire Press for originally publishing the work in this collection in book form. Also, thanks to Guild Literary Complex, the Poetry Foundation, the OSU-Tulsa Center for Poets & Writers and the Holland Hall School community.

Extra special thanks to my poetry teachers and mentors: Miss Gwendolyn Brooks, Dr. Haki R. Madhubuti, Marilyn Nelson, Dr. Reginald Gibbons, Sharon Olds, Mark Doty, Afaa M. Weaver, Hannibal B. Johnson and the late, great Galway Kinnell and Phillip Levine.

Extra extra special thanks to Rilla Askew, Roger Bonair-Agard, Dr. Randall Horton, Major Jackson, Tyehimba Jess, A. Van Jordan, Toni Asante Lightfoot, Adrian Matejka and Patricia Smith for relentless love and support.